KNOW YOUR PT BOAT

HIGGINS PT

ISSUED BY

THE BUREAU OF SHIPS

TECHNICAL PUBLICATION NO. 9

©2010 Periscope Film LLC
All Rights Reserved
ISBN #978-1-935700-17-3
www.PeriscopeFilm.com

RESTRICTED

PUBLICATIONS
in the
"T. P." SERIES

T. P.—1, Pointers on Boiler Operation

T. P.—2, Pointers On Turbine Operation

T. P.—3, Pointers on Steam Systems and Their Auxiliaries

T. P.—4, Get Your Bearings Straight

T. P.—5, Hang On To Your Line

T. P.—6, Pointers on Shipboard Ventilation

T. P.—8, Pointers on Damage Control

T. P.—9, Know Your PT Boat

T. P.—10, Shallow Water Diving

T. P.—11, Pointers on Traveling to Toyko
 (Save That Fuel Oil)

IN PRODUCTION

T. P.—12, About Requisitions

T. P.—13, About Clean Oil

T. P.—14, Pointers on Safe Shipbuilding and Repair
 (Personal Safety)

T. P.—15, Pointers on Fire Fighting

T. P.—16, Take Care of Your Ship's Salvage Equipment

PUBLISHED BY
BUREAU OF SHIPS

NAVY DEPARTMENT
BUREAU OF SHIPS

Washington, 15 July 1945

Though a comparatively new weapon in naval warfare, PTs have operated in every theatre of war and have proven themselves an important part of the fleet.

The object of TP-9 "Know Your PT Boat" is to bring information and hints to acquaint new PT personnel with the ships on which they are to serve.

E. L. COCHRANE,
Vice Admiral, USN
Chief, Bureau of Ships

INDOCTRINATION

Now don't get scared. Sure, it's a big word and it means plenty. It means *PT Doctrine*—the "red hot" dope about the boats for Y-O-U from those who know. PT Doctrine, unlike others, is seldom dry—nothing connected with PTs is dry for long.

Like every man-o'-war, a PT is made for only one purpose:

*To Meet the Enemy and Destroy Him
Wherever He Can Be Found*

This little booklet is to help you achieve that one purpose.

WHAT IS A PT BOAT?

Very much like fire, your PT can be your best friend or worst enemy. It will be your friend only if you know your boat. The first enemy you will encounter is ignorance—your ignorance about PTs. Kill your ignorance at every opportunity. It is the first step in killing the enemy. The paramount rule is: *Know Your BOAT*.

A PT is the fastest warship afloat. Its features of speed and knockout power have been ballyhooed in the press, not without reason. A PT can and has taken on everything from canoes to battleships. Enemy tanks and trucks also appear on the tally sheet. Shooting down enemy planes has been one of the most satisfying tasks. So, whether the enemy be within reach on or under the sea, on the land, or in the air, a PT will attack. Be proud of your boat. Make yours the best. But to be proud of it you must know what it is made of and what it can do. Don't forget, it is a fine weapon, but only the weapon, while you are the warrior who through your knowledge can make it a valuable asset.

Of plywood and mahogany construction, a PT is light yet strong, lightly armored yet strongly armed. Its draft is seldom over 6 feet thus enabling it to maneuver in shallow water. Details on the boat's construction are given on page 357, MTB Manual, 1943. If you are in doubt as to the purpose or usage of a piece of equipment, don't hesitate to ask. Ignorance is no excuse.

DON'T STAY STUMPED

BOAT—TOPSIDE

General.—From stem to stern do not overlook an item. See, feel, and think about every piece of equipment on the boat. Useful thinking can earn you a rate. A PT is different from any other man-of-war in that every man aboard must know his boat from stern to stem. See, feel, and know the operation, maintenance, and purpose of every piece of equipment on the boat.

Don't be like one boot who ducked down inside his "armored" turret during an attack and then later when he discovered that the turret was made of ¾" plywood he fainted. We aren't blaming him for being scared but we are blaming him for not knowing his boat. This incident may strike you as funny but other cases of ignorance have proven fatal.

Bullnose.—The bullnose is used to run your lines through when at anchor, moored alongside another boat, or when moored alongside a dock. When at anchor the bullnose will keep the bow of the boat facing the wind and at all times it will keep the lines from chafing against the side of the boat.

Cleats.—Cleats are used to secure mooring lines to. Keep plenty of slack in all mooring lines. Three loose lag screws, a heavy strain, and bingo—you've lost a cleat.

Anchor.—The anchor provided to PT boats are light weight (50 pounds) and are designed to have far greater holding power than the old style anchor. However, to get the highest holding power of the anchor you must pay out enough line to do the job. Take a sounding before dropping the hook (anchor). Under normal wind and sea conditions and on a hard mud or sand bottom, a scope of seven times the depth of the water will be adequate. If the wind, sea, or tide increase slack out more line.

Navigation Lights.—Must be maintained in perfect order so they will operate when required and will not accidentally illuminate at an inopportune time. Never give the enemy a light to shoot at. There were several instances where PT blinker and signal lights flashed on while in enemy territory. Hence, it is urged that proper care be taken, particularly in keeping switches and wiring dry and waterproofed.

"PARDON ME"

Search Light: Be sure the "safety", provided in the circuit, is in good condition and is in the "off" position except when in use (to preclude accidental lighting). It can be very embarrassing.

Towing Gear.—Also called "bridle and pendant". Keep it in good shape. Grease your wire rope and shackles. Paint the towing eye or ring to prevent corrosion and rust. You can't paddle or sail a crippled PT with any degree of speed or accuracy. Towing rigs have saved boats and men many times in the combat areas. You will learn to depend on it.

Canopy.—A large canvas, which looks like a sheik's desert abode, covers the forecastle in the manner of a huge tent. It is the joy and comfort of every boat in off-patrol hours. Waterproof it. Camouflage it. Roll it up when stowing it, rather than creasing it, for creases make it crack and soon you have a leaky, uncomforting canopy.

Toe Rail.—Is used for securing fenders and cargo net. It is a necessity in tying down the boat awning while at anchor. Prisoners can be secured to it, thus making the forecastle an ideal brig.

Sampson Post.—Is indispensable in anchoring. Like the bullnose, never allow it to get loose. If you lack a towing bridle the sampson post will suffice.

Atop Charthouse and Day Room.—Neither place is a promenade. Both are waterproofed with but a thin sheet of airplane cloth. Rips and weak spots should be patched promptly. A leaky charthouse impairs navigation, ruins charts, and may damage your radio gear.

Cockpit.—This "flying bridge" is the center of the boat. It has or should have the following items in and around it:

Blackout Light: An on-and-off switch secured to the hatch. It cuts off the charthouse lights whenever the cockpit hatch is opened, provided that the proper chartroom switch has been thrown. Traffic through the chart house should be held to a minimum. Below decks is accessible through several other hatches.

Panel Cover: A square piece of canvas which can be neatly rolled over the instruments to protect them from water and sunlight. Sunlight weakens and fades the phosphorous dials. Also it covers the glass which glares in the moonlight.

CO_2 Release: For the Lux fire-extinguishing system. KNOW WHERE IT IS!

Black Light: Is the only exposed light topside that is turned on during patrol. Its ultraviolet rays served to illuminate the phosphorous letters and numerals on the instrument panel. Its limited range of visibility makes it ideal for night work.

Cockpit Seat: Just abaft the wheel, is ideal for the footsore.

Megaphone: Keep it handy and ready for shouting orders or for listening for planes and other craft. Carry at least two megaphones. Megaphone communication between boats in a section should be used to minimize radio transmissions.

Antenna.—Will freeze into one solid rod if you do not lubricate it and exercise its sections. When your boat is going into the A-frame (drydock of a PT tender) the antenna is lowered. On patrol, it is ordinarily best to use maximum height. One radio operator is credited with a Jap plane for that reason. The plane came in so low that he hit the whip antenna and before he could recover from the jolt he plopped into the sea. Of course, it is best not to rely on your antenna to knock down planes, but it has happened. Another thing—lookouts take notice—*never touch the antenna*, especially in damp weather. During a transmission, it is a veritable powerhouse. No transmissions or receptions can be carried out successfully while you are in contact with the antenna. Brace yourself with the hand rails provided and not with the antenna.

"SHOCKING EH WHAT?"

Fantail.—Here is a section of the boat that is multi-purpose. It is a place for work and play. Swimming and fishing over the stern are great pastimes. Just as the gunners use the forecastle for most of their work, the engineers stick to the fantail with theirs. Also everybody has clothes to wash. The fantail is the best place for this, but do not use the ammunition boxes as scrub boards. Another thing, you will want to keep your boat's sides clean of lye stain. This stain can be prevented by tacking a six-foot lathe along each gunwale. This will form a little lip or gutter and will take all your wash water over the stern.

Lookout Positions.—Are posted at the discretion of the boat captain. Naturally, they should be complete with each lookout covering a definite sector. Never leave a sector unguarded especially when picking up prisoners. Lookouts must report all things seen and get an acknowledgment ("Very Well") from the conning officer. Repeat the report until you do get an acknowledgment. Everyone on the boat should practice "distance judging" both night and day. Compare your guesses with the charted distances of buoys or points of land. Remember, the enemy may attack or that challenges often come from abaft the beam. That is because he usually sees your wake before he sees your boat. Do not concentrate attention on flares. Flares are dropped to silhouette you. The attack will likely come from the direction 180° from the flares. Cover all sectors.

"STAB IN THE BACK DUE"

Vents.—Not to be used as cleats. Straining fenders and lines secured to them will rip them off easily. Stuffing rags and clothes in them will make them useless, especially in the engine room. Engines, like men, need air.

Dead Lights.—Are the ports which give light below decks and cannot be opened. Heavy objects dropped on them, such as gun barrels and magazines, will crack the glass and induce serious leaks in the overhead. Lacking replacement, use plexiglass cut from chart house ports. Since these ports are usually boarded up to insure blackout, the plexiglas can be removed and made to serve many such useful purposes.

Speaking Tube: An intercom between the cockpit and the charthouse.

Cockpit Scupper: Do not sweep dirt down this drain. The deck of the cockpit should be kept clean. Dirt from the cockpit has often clogged this drain.

Compass Cover: Made of canvas, the cover serves to protect the compass face and mechanism from the elements during off-patrol periods.

Torpedo Director: Can be used as a pelorus for taking relative bearings as well as for its primary use. It should be stowed below when not on patrol.

Torpedo Tools: Keep these tools in plain view and within reach of the torpedoes. Everyone should know how to stop a HOT RUN. Get your instructions. If a hot run cannot be stopped, run to the bow of the boat. An unarmed warhead will not explode.

Lockers: For stowage of MP (Multi-Purpose) light, blinker gun, and batteries (dry cells). Other signal devices can be stowed here. *Always keep recognition gear ready and in reach.*

ARMAMENT.—Treated in the GQ Drill Section.

Auxiliary Deck Cells.—
1. When not in use should be carefully folded and stowed in a dark cool place. Gear should not be piled or stowed on top of them.
2. When in use, be sure they are not in contact with sharp projections on the deck and protect them from chafing and puncture.

BOAT—BELOW DECKS

Head.—Use it right. Pumps are difficult to get. Be sure the valve is shut after the bowl is flushed or else you will start to ship water. An open-head pump underway is like having a hole in your bottom. This space is also a good spot in which to stow canned goods and your spare anchor, as well as spare soap and toilet tissue.

Crew's Quarters.—This will be your home. Take care of it. A well-painted deck usually will keep it dry. Don't forget to look under the lower deck plates. You may be carrying an aquarium around and not know it except that your boat will be slow and loggy. Electrolysis will eat holes in the pipe carrying salt water to the head. Inspect the pipe carefully, especially after your boat has been in commission over 8 months. A small undetected leak will fill your bilges in a short time and wreck vital equipment installed there. Learn the connections and valves. They are few in number and easily understood.

Gunnery Locker.—This is a spacious cubby hole located about amidships. The gunners are gradually being forced out, but it still is the ideal place for stowage of gun barrels and other spares, as well as for small arms. It is a dry, clean spot and accommodates much ammunition. It is better to stow gunnery and torpedo tools topside in a watertight 20-mm. box. Many boats have added this feature to the fantail of the boat. The tools are more accessible and the bulkheads below decks will be much cleaner. Many gunners think the bulkheads are "pay chits". Hence, the many fingerprints often found there.

Charthouse.—Within the charthouse are the vitals of the boat. From here the movement of the boat is directed, hence it is the brains of the boat. The equipment it contains need not be listed here. The RM and QM should be well acquainted with their tools and so should the rest of the crew. A few points will be made here as to the use of some items.

Like any engine, machine, or apparatus, the equipment in the charthouse was made to be operated. Hence, it must be used to give efficient operation. If it is not used (like a man who doesn't take exercise) it gets sluggish and functions poorly, if at all. Remember that a PT is exposed to moisture from both the sea and the atmosphere. All equipment should be run at least 15 minutes a day. This exercising will limber up the parts and dry them as well. To combat moisture from spray, watertight overhead and bulkheads cannot be allowed to wear or leak. Patch cracks and ruptures in the fabric promptly.

Galley.—Here is where the "cook" heats up the cans. A PT galley is much more than that. It can and has turned out American, Italian, French, Chinese, and even Japanese cuisine. Pies, cookies, and cakes flow from this modernistic kitchen if you've got a happy cook. Your refrigerator can make ice cream, ice cubes, and frozen delights (especially good is frozen fruit cup). Once a Jap bullet punctured a refrigerator unit and drained it of all its freon. Several of the boats then decided to put armor plate about the refrigerator. So you see it's really very important, for it contributes to the living comforts which are all too few in the Area. Your refrigerator pump and motor need servicing. Don't let them wear down or overheat. To keep meat, your refrigerator must be in top shape. It is rare to have fresh meat and when issued it comes in 100-pound quantities. Hence the necessity for a good freeze or reefer. Have a drip pan properly placed or the meat juices will leak into the bilges and in a week you'll be accused of carrying a dead Jap around in your bilges.

GALLEY GUARD

A bit of advice about the cook. He's likely to be temperamental and have his moods. He needs help at meal time. So keep him in good humor by mess cooking without griping and helping him get supplies. He may serve you breakfast in bed some morning. Generally, he's a good gunner, too. You'll learn to count on "cookie."

The galley stove with all its attachments and source of power must be known by everyone. Above all, *remember to have your generator running and galley switch "on", when the stove is operated.* Also bear in mind that finding and destroying the enemy is more important than a hot pot of Joe. So don't gripe if the galley must be secured to give the needed juice to the radio equipment.

In temperate zones and especially in the Tropics any food particles left about will attract insects and bugs. Cockroach races are swell to watch but not when the race course is your bread box. Aerosol bombs are used to fumigate the galley effectively.

The galley pump is the most used and abused pump aboard. It is probably the only one you will ever have. Be sure the packing is tight and that you do not pump while the faucet is closed. Water on any naval vessel is valuable. So also on a PT which is often based on an island with no fresh-water supply. A leaky fresh-water pump will mean a serious loss.

Garbage disposal appears to be a simple procedure on a PT but there are rules. Don't clutter up the beaches near your anchorage with tin cans. Punch holes in them. The best method is to dump garbage overboard at sea, taking care that cans are punctured. Guard against the loss of your garbage can. It's usually allowed to hang over the side to soak out. Don't forget to pick it up when your boat gets underway. It's wise to make a complete circuit inspection of the boat, just prior to getting underway, checking for fenders, buckets, hoses, clothes, and lines that will foul the screws.

Day Room.—A large place which can accommodate four bunks easily, and another sack set up in the center temporarily. A half-dozen army-style cots should be carried to accommodate sleepers topside. The day room is usually taken over by the engineers. They often make it into an ideal clubhouse except that *smoking is absolutely prohibited in the day room.*

Self-Sealing Tanks.—Points to make note of on self-sealing tanks:
1. If checking cell's interior through the inspection door—*wear a respirator!* Make certain tank compartment is well ventilated. Always have someone stand by. The toxic fumes from gas are dangerous.
2. Observe inspection periods and procedures.
3. In case of puncture or suspicion of damage to a cell, have it inspected and repaired within 72 hours by a competent repairman.

Notes for Quartermaster.—
1. Keep charts in order, clean, and do not erase reefs or allow water to eradicate them. Your dividers are to pick off distances with and not to prick holes in the charts. Plot courses well clear of navigational dangers. The charts can be wrong in their location of reefs. In particular, stay well clear of river deltas. Many times they are not on your charts, and deltas are forever growing, shifting, and extending themselves.

2. Learn your recognition procedure cold. Have the correct recognition equipment in perfect condition and at hand. *Effective recognition signals must be known at all times.* Remember the times of signal changes.

3. Get the feel of the lead line at night and be able to yell out the soundings loud and clear.

4. Practice your signalling (semaphore and blinker).

5. Learn all the charthouse jobs of the other rates.

6. Dry cells must be kept dry. Some day you may have to use them to help start the generator.

7. All parts of the Flux Gate Compass must be insured against disturbance and moisture. It is a magnetic compass and must be free of disturbances and loose gear such as guns and engine parts. Check cables and plugs occasionally for corrosion. Like the radio gear, operate it daily. It should be operated uncaged at all times under way.

8. Keep binoculars in good shape. Don't rub off the blue tint. It aids you in night vision. Excessive heat is not good for this type of binocular, so keep them out of the sun. The importance of these glasses cannot be overestimated. From captured Japanese documents, it is clear that our glasses are better than theirs. The Japs complain and admit in official correspondence that we saw them long before they saw us, chiefly because we have the better glasses. Don't give away this advantage by having dirty, wet, or shattered binoculars. Keep them clean, dry, and safe. Clamp down on the boots who go down hatches with a binocular dangling from their necks. Many glasses have been shattered in this way and replacements are almost unobtainable.

Notes for Engineers.—While the charthouse has the vitals, the engine room contains the guts. It is too technical and large a subject to be covered here, yet some suggestions are in order:

1. The puncturing of your gas tanks is not usually the cause for explosion. Rather it is the gas fumes that erupt from around the hole in your tank which are dangerous. Gas vapor is what you have to fear most. You don't need much to make the proper mixture for an explosion.

2. Everyone should know where the important switches are, such as for the radio, galley, refrigerator, main feed, etc.

3. Knowing how to start the engines and generator is another all-around job for everyone. The generator is a luxury as well as a necessity. Without a "Jennie" you can't cook or use the refrigerator. Also your most important chartroom equipment needs the steady and reliable source of current it puts out.

4. The operation of self-bailers is very simple. They function at medium high speed when the valve is opened. The valve should be closed when not under way. There is usually one self-bailer on every watertight bulkhead. It is essential to keep the engine room dry for the batteries must not be permitted to ground out.

5. Have on hand some wooden plugs for stopping up bullet and shrapnel holes. Rubber plugs are also very helpful for jagged holes in the stacks, exhaust manifolds, and other lines carrying water, oil, and gasoline.

6. Don't stuff clothes or rags in the vents. The engines as well as the engineer need plenty of air.

7. Keep the sound phones in good shape. You never know when your enunciators will go haywire.

8. Engineers should use the small portable Romec electric pump for draining bilges, transferring oil from barrel to tanks, cleaning out gas tanks, and flushing down generally when in port. A good length of hose is also invaluable.

9. Don't lean or rest your foot on the shifting lever. You are burning out the clutch throw-out collar. Don't slam the shifting lever in and out. A steady push or pull will lengthen the life of the reverse gear and save you work.

10. Remember, *maintenance is much easier than overhaul and repair!* Do little things first when you are losing r. p. m., such as checking plugs or loose wires instead of tearing down reverse gears, etc. There is a schedule of inspection set up which if followed will save trouble. These checks cannot be made from the engine-room hatch.

11. Sniff for gas fumes, particularly when starting the engines. Engineers should do this instinctively, but often other rates must start the engines. So everyone must be on the alert for fumes. Practice this precaution: *Sniff for Fumes!* Use the bilge exhaust blower before starting engines if such a blower is installed on your boat.

12. Your cleaning of gas and oil filters periodically is one key to good operation Only by close watch over engines and related equipment can you discover small leaks in the water, fuel, and oil lines.

13. Small apertures in your lines occur usually at the joints and couplings. Keep these tight. A small hole will be enough to allow a little gas to spurt out, create fumes and consequently an explosion and fire. Too many men have been killed and injured because of this hazard. Keep close watch on your gas lines.

14. Engine operating instructions are covered in the "Packard Operating Manual" and the "Packard 4M-2500 Marine Engine Construction Operation and Servicing Manual." The latter contains a wealth of information and is well illustrated. A lot of time, money and effort has been expended on these books. Get acquainted with them Highly skilled technical engineers are continually working to improve the design and performance of your engines so don't try to redesign them yourself—such as changing engine timing. Performance curves prove the books are right. Your job is to operate engines according to the instruction books.

15. Keep your engines clean inside and out. A dirty engine or engine room is usually the sign of a lax engineer, and soon results in failure of the equipment.

16. The instrument panel tells the story of engine performance. Watch the gasoline, oil and water temperatures, and pressures. Keep them within the limits recommended by the manufacturer.

17. Study your manifold pressure curves in relation to engine rpm and at no time exceed these values. There is a handy operating manual which can be used to good advantage. Keep your manifold gauges running equally. Your manifold gauge measures the amount of work being done by the engine. Make each engine do its equal share of work.

18. Do not overwork your boat by useless jockeying. You must nurse it and be considerate of your engines if you want the best out of them in emergencies. Whooping along at 2500 rpm when there is no need for it is slap happy operation.

19. Great attention must be paid to gas leaks both inside and outside of the engine. Another check for leaks besides sniffing and looking, is this: Feel the fuel pump drain tube. If this tube is cool while the engine is running it is probable that your fuel pump seal is leaking. This will hold no great danger while the engine is running; but when the engine is secured, gas will seep into the crankcase which may cause explosion and fire when you next start the engine. Don't forget, a cold drain tube is usually the best indication of a leaking fuel pump seal. This operational casualty is explained quite fully in the "Packard Maintenance Manual, Bulletin," #17, 1-19-43. Other such valuable bits of information are contained in this manual. Make use of them. Study them. Only through them can you know your engine room. Some of the latest engine operation dope can be obtained from the "Bureau of Ships News Letter—Motor Torpedo Boats" which appears at irregular intervals.

Notes for Radiomen.—

1. Stow your phones and mikes in a dry place. Make a receptacle or canvas cover for the bridge phones and mikes for they are most likely to become wet. Dry this gear out at the base after every patrol.

2. Be clear and concise.

3. Transmit as little as possible to expedite traffic, to reduce confusion, and to avoid enemy interception and RDF tracking.

4. Do not make a radio check when leaving for patrol. If every boat checked on each patrol, the enemy could easily count the number of boats on patrol and learn the strength of the base.

5. Check your frequencies often and calibrate properly.

6. Learn correct procedure.

7. Know your alternate frequencies and when to use them. Jamming by the enemy is certainly to be expected, so be prepared for it.

8. Your VHF is not as secure as you perhaps assume. Transmissions over VHF have gone 400 to 500 miles beyond the horizon. PTs operating reasonably close to enemy territory or units can give away their position and valuable information by useless chatter over a VHF circuit. And remember, you are not the only pebble on the beach. Our planes use it extensively. Unnecessary PT transmissions must not clutter up communications of a vital operating aircraft squadron. You may think the air is clear because you do not hear any transmissions, but, remember, they may be receiving you several hundred miles away where they may be making a strike. So do not depend on the term "line-of-sight" transmissions. It is not reliable at all times, *hence guard the use of your VHF set much as you do the TCS.* Jam sessions, razzle-dazzle cowboy stuff, and hot-shot vocalizing are all very amusing to you if you are a lunk head. Just consider the harm you can do to yourself, your shipmates, and our aviators and you will be sure to knock off all unnecessary transmissions. Even when another boat in your section cannot hear you, your transmissions may carry to out-of-sight areas where the enemy may be listening.

Transmission security for both radios is greatly enhanced by the use of follow-the-leader tactics, basic formations, and courses established before leaving the base, and prearranged rendezvous points and times if the boats get separated. When PTs operate in sight of land, special care must be taken in VHF transmission. The Japs have many monitor stations on land and they have made many experiments with VHF type of equipment. It is to be expected that they are aware of our approximate frequencies. Give a Jap station enough transmissions and a shore battery will be laying a shell in your cockpit. For valuable aids in operation and on your equipment see MTB Communication Manual, 1944.

Lazarette.—Used for storage of gear. One of the most important features here is the auxiliary steering apparatus. Know where the linkage is and how to rig the auxiliary tiller. Keep loose gear—such as oil cans—clear of rudders and steering gear. Oil and paint cans have been known to jam the steering at critical moments. The Navy maxim, "Keep It Clean", is not just for appearance's sake, but more important, for safety's sake.

Watertight Hatches.—Hatches must be dogged down. Particularly important is the hatch between lazarette and engine room. A screw thrown through your bottom will fill up your lazarette in short order. Holes in the stacks will pour water into this compartment. Leaky rudder post packing can let in quantities of water.

BOAT—GENERAL MAINTENANCE

The four strong men of your boat's structure are rivets, bolts, screws, and glue—and don't let anyone kid you about the glue—it's strong. So long as each one of these members is doing its job the integral strength of the PT hull structure can be maintained. When one lets down, one of the others has to take added strain and eventually weakens. Under heavy going a minor weakness may develop into major damage.

Note, too, any splits you may see in any part of the boat's structure and call them to the attention of your boat officer. After heavy weather missions, collisions, or severe jolts against a dock or shipside you may find much to report. Cracks in paint around structural members will show movement.

"A taut ship is a happy ship," but there is no ship that will become "untaut" quicker than a PT if you neglect her. You must watch her if you want to keep her taut. You can't keep her from working, but you can keep her from breaking up. For example, a split bulkhead can be strengthened by battens; joints can be stiffened by setting up on bolts or rivets. You have plans of your boat on board which will show the fastenings. Use your plans for minor repairs by ship's force. If you follow this procedure you may save an eventual major job by a base force. Note, however, that taking up on fastenings must be done all at once—*in one session—and when waterborne.*

When tanks, engines, or other equipment are removed and the boat skeleton is exposed, look for signs of weakness; look also for dry rot, the ogre of all wooden vessels in poorly ventilated compartments. Remove the ogre and replace with new wood and plenty of wood preservative.

Keep your vessel well painted. Don't let the weather get in. A brush full of paint today will keep disintegration away tomorrow. Keep your paint thinned down. Two light coats are better than one heavy coat, and that goes double for the bottom paint, too. Thick, heavy coats will blister and crack.

You boat's speed depends to a great extent on the bottom condition. You may have a slow number and not know by just looking at her. Rub her down and speed her up.

Speed losses up to 15 knots have been reported as a result of foul bottoms. If she's slimy to the touch she needs a scrubbing. You don't have to haul out to get the slime off. A long-handled, stiff-bristled brush will do the job.

About Fueling

Melville doesn't want to have for its motto, "Our Graduates are spread all over the earth" so here's how you can help. If you ever spill any gasoline overboard while fueling or during any other work don't even *think* of starting your engines, main or auxiliary, until the boat is towed away from that spot or until the wind and the sea dissipate the gasoline. The tendency is for the gasoline to accumulate around the hull, particularly the mufflers. There is one case on record where they had to sweep up the pieces of what once had been a bee-utiful PT because some lunkhead started his engines while floating in the middle of that 100 octane stuff. And if you see gasoline around another boat, don't just sit around waiting to see things pop—find one of the boat officers and tell him about it. Four very serious PT boat fires directly attributable to improperly handled gasoline have recently occurred, so geez, fellows, try to be careful 'cause it's no fun to be spread all over the earth with that gal back in Fall River awaitin'.

DRILLS

How to fight a PT is a great study. It's like Emily Post in Reversia, or courtesy turned inside out. You invite Hirohito to a duck dinner and he ends up cooking his own goose. Like Commander K. did one night. After expending all his "fish" and ammunition, he ran down the narrow alley of the enemy convoy and had the Japs lobbing shells at each other. Of course, there are better ways of feasting on Japs than that but before you can set yourself down to one of those exciting and pleasurable repasts you have to know the "etiquette" of such a banquet.

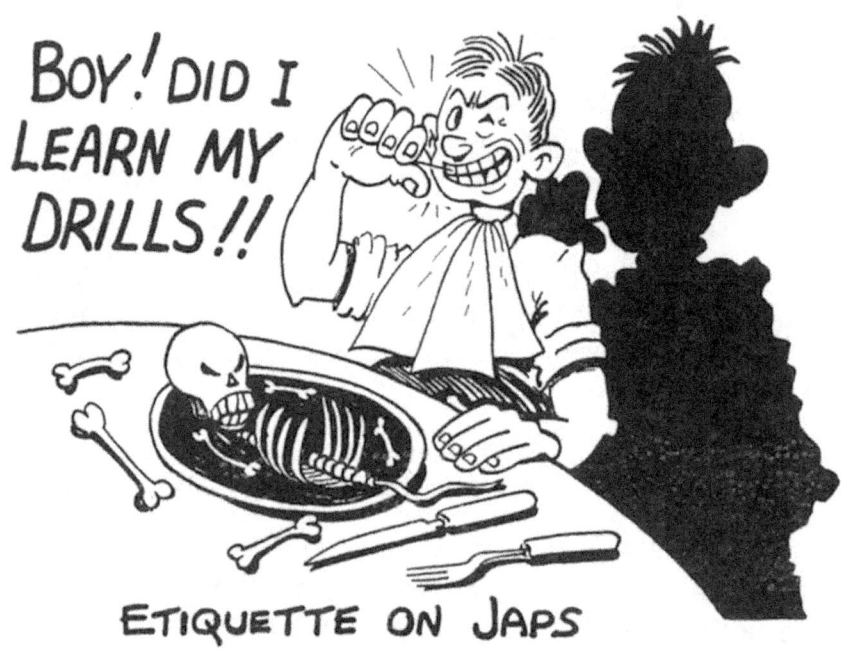

ETIQUETTE ON JAPS

Remarkably vivid descriptions of how, where, and when to enjoy such feasts are given in confidential publications available to you. They are written by men recently returned. But first comes some necessary dope concerning those drills that always seem so dull. Maybe if you knew that "Ace" Eddie Rickenbacker greased and fitted every shell before he ever fired, you would begin to look on your gun, drills, and routine checks as your best friends. So, on to the drills and see what they have meant to others and what they can mean to you.

Three drills will be covered here:

    1. General Quarters Drill.
    2. Fire Drill.
    3. Abandon Ship Drill.

GENERAL QUARTERS DRILL

When you have your own boat your GQ Station will be well known to you, so there is no need to rehearse the various positions. Know your spot and be there. Aside from the actual firing of the guns the important thing is the *preparation*. Everything must be in perfect operating order. "Be Prepared" is not just a Boy Scout motto, it is the watchword of every fighting ship. You can make no excuses to the Japs for a jammed 50, a weak drive spring, or a 20-mm. magazine with no tension on it. The guns must fire when you want them. They will, only if you have done your drills so that you can do everything automatically. Strip your guns regularly, exercise the springs, and make other routine checks. Then you will know in times of action how to put tension on a magazine and how to blind load. You cannot use flashlights on deck in the Area. Keep those guns in shape by learning your drills and routines now. The same with your "fish" ("torpedoes", to the landlubber), the smoke-screen generator, and the depth charges.

The notes following cover most of the armament carried on the boats and an account is given of the experience had with this gear. Take this advice and value it, for it is the Voice of Experience:

37-mm. Gun.—To the "Barge Hunters" this is a fondly loved gun. Its flexibility, ease of firing, destructive power, and flat trajectory make it a grand gun against targets at moderate range. A 37-mm. seldom jams of itself. The few jams that do occur are usually traced to faulty ammunition. The hints given here will acquaint you with the methods used in combat areas to make this the terror antibarge gun:

1. Test fire each batch of ammunition. Check the primers for obvious defects and particularly note how tightly the casing holds the projectile. Loose projectiles can be fired, but they will be short on range and lacking in accuracy.

2. Always try to get the latest issue of 37-mm. shells. Stow it carefully, well lubricated and in a watertight box. Air frequently, for shells are subject to "sweating."

3. Loaded magazines are easily sprung from the jarring movement of the boat. Unload the magazine when returning to base. Also keep it unloaded on the way to your patrol station.

4. Correct loading is very important. The primer end of the shell must be snug against the magazine—*push them aft.*

5. The loader should continuously tell the gunner how many rounds he has left so that the gunner can keep his eyes glued to the target. Likewise, the loader should keep the magazine as full as possible so that weight will be evenly distributed and the gun will be fed steadily.

6. Carry spare screws for the magazine.

7. The belt in the magazine should not be drum tight but neither should it be visibly slack.

8. Don't full load the gun until signal is given.

9. Check bore for "clean bore." Covers or rags in the barrel have caused explosions while firing, so be sure such things are removed before firing. These projectiles are very sensitive.

10. In firing, the lock frame must be fully forward. Recock, if it is not or cannot be pushed fully forward. Do not pull lock frame to the rear except as a last resort. Charging the gun is dangerous for normally the projectile will pull free from the casing.

11. The gun is easily maintained. Cleaning and light oiling of the barrel and block are all the servicing required.

12. The U-shaped connection should be facing up and the safety catch must be on the outboard side.

13. Lock the barrel correctly.

14. Left and right drive rods are not interchangeable. Keep oil at the proper level in the recuperating cylinder—use only U. S. Army Spec. No. 2–36D.

15. Oil for cleaning can be either 2110 or 2190.

16. Both AP and HE have tracer. Good results have been had with a ratio of 1 AP and 3 HE.

40-mm Gun.—This gun is best operated with 4 men but 3 men can do a good job. It is a wonderful gun for both AA and surface fire. It seldom jams. The prime point to remember is load the shells at the proper angle— nose canted downward.

20-mm. Gun.—This gun is so powerful that it has earned the name "cannon." When you hit something with a 20-mm., you really do some damage. Not small punctures but gaping holes are the marks left on the enemy by this powerful shell. Aside from the usual preparation and care of a 20-mm., the following are helpful hints:

1. Precaution must be taken in clearing a 20-mm. jam. Always have a bucket of water on hand. When a jam occurs, souse the breech and barrel. If you cannot get the projectile out in a few seconds, secure the gun for about 5 minutes. In any case, never stick your nose or fingers into the breech. Keep clear and use your ram rod.

2. Practice cocking of the 20-mm. It is a tricky operation and should be done speedily and with ease, especially in the dark. It is the only way to clear a jam, and to get the gun set to fire again.

3. The loader must get a rhythm in his task and eliminate groping at night. The gunner and loader who drill in the daylight with their eyes closed are doing a wise thing. The magazine is quite heavy. On a high trunnion gun, the loader should be both strong and tall.

ALL TENSE BUT THE MAGAZINE

4. Be sure that prior to any imminent action all magazines are *on full tension at 60 pounds*. If your magazines have been in use a long time, it is wise to pull out a few rounds before loading, but be sure you still have on the full tension. This precaution will give the last few rounds in your magazine an extra push and will prevent jamming.

5. Practice all operations, especially cocking and loading, in the dark or with your eyes closed. This type of practice, "blind cocking and blind loading" is invaluable. A PT operates chiefly at night and any kind of illumination of deck is taboo. Get the feel of the gun, the magazine, their every part and get the rhythm in cocking, loading, and firing.

30-Cal. Cockpit Gun.—The "pea shooter" is a very light gun carrying a great amount of tracer ammunition. This gun may be operated by an officer or gunner on the bridge. It is very much like a 50-cal. gun in looks and operation. It can have single or double barrels operation.

Twin 50s.—These are as familiar armament to a PT as its fish. The port and starboard turrets characterize the deadly sting that can be unleashed against air and surface targets. They are sensitive guns and their machined parts must be well lubricated and kept free of corrosion. The guns in a turret, like a team of horses, must function together in order to give accuracy of fire. A 50 turret in good shape should not jam for long. The essential points to remember are:

1. If it jams, *Charge It, Charge It!* Do this at least twice before you even think of looking for serious trouble or stripping your gun.

2. Every gun has it peculiarities. Learn them and make allowances. When disassembling, keep each gun and its parts together rather than tossing them into a common stock pile.

3. Ammunition must be clean and well covered. Protect it against dirt and water. Oiled or greased cartridges should not be fired. Oil or grease causes the collection of dust and other abrasives which may be injurious to the gun and also may result in hazardous chamber pressures. Dust, dirt, fibers, and even hair may cause your gun to jam. Salt water corrodes the cases and moisture can make your primers useless.

4. Oil buffers on both guns should be closely teamed for synchronized firing.

5. Head space must be accurately set.

6. Have good strong drive springs.

7. Strong springs should be kept in your feed pawls.

8. Do not follow through with the charging handle or try to push it back to "in battery" position. Instead, pull back on the handle again and try to clear the jam that way. Forcing will make the jam worse. When it is necessary to lift the cover piece, do not stick your fingers or face into the breech. Have a screw driver handy with which to do your poking around. Nature does not grow new noses or new eyes or new fingers. This precaution is particularly applicable with a 20-mm gun. It is preferable to use your ram rod first with both guns.

Know Your Gun.—Many hours of leisure will be yours on the boats. This time spent learning your guns and cleaning your ammunition will mean plenty when action comes your way. *The actual shooting of your gun at an enemy is comparatively infinitesimal.* Like a certain kind of soap which is 99 44/100% pure, good shooting is 99 44/100% pure preparation. Eddie Rickenbacker, World War ace pilot, realized this. While his buddies smoked and played poker all the time, Rickenbacker used to check every cartridge for his guns. He used to lubricate them and fit each one into the chamber of the gun it was to be fired from. Such painstaking preparation was the reason that he piled up his high toll of German planes and is the reason why he came back alive. The same can be true of you. Your life and the lives of your shipmates will depend on your zeal in having your guns in not *good*—but in *perfect* shape.

KNOW YOUR GUN

Depth Charges.—Though seldom used, they are always good passengers to have along. These demons of the deep can be used against both surface craft and subs. Squadron X in the Solomons effectively scared a Jap destroyer that was bearing down on a PT by using a depth charge. Who knows when a Jap sub will pop up? So, keep them handy and ready.

Smoke Generator.—Both an offensive and defensive asset—smoke confuses the enemy. Here is some good stuff to remember on your smoke generator:

1. Open valve wide (3 full turns) when in operation. Let the time nozzles control your density of smoke.
2. Close tightly after use.
3. Clean pipe, valve, and nozzles with fresh water after use.
4. Rubber tip must cover the nozzle at all times. The pressure of the smoke will blow it off. This is important for the pipe, nozzles, and valve will be clogged from chemical activity if free air is permitted to enter when the generator is not in use.

Mortar.—Keep it covered, and when firing be sure to have the bore clear of rags, water, and muzzle cover. It is chiefly used for illumination and shore bombardment.

Rockets.—Rockets are coming into use more and more each day. Little can be said about them here for security reasons. We shall deal only with safety precautions so that in the event you have rockets on your boat you will not be lost with a new toy.

1. Don't keep rockets aboard your boat while the boat is tied up at the dock for repairs. Accidents can and do happen. The rockets when disassembled are a very dangerous fire hazard. When assembled and lying about and ignited, the results would probably be tragic.

2. When fired, rockets produce a large blast effect to the rear. The danger zone to the rear may be as great as 200 feet rearward and 150° either side of the line of aim. Stay well clear of them when they are being fired, loaded, or unloaded.

3. A rocket round when assembled is self-propulsive, and if accidentally ignited will attain its full velocity and the fuse will arm in less than one second. Keep the rounds disassembled whenever possible. When the projectile and rocket motor are separated, the rocket motor is non-propulsive and is only considered a fire hazard.

4. Should rocket launchers be installed on your boat, you will be equipped with a firing panel for firing the rockets. A safety plug is secured to the side of the firing panel by a safety chain. The safety plug must be removed from the firing panel and in the possession of the person carrying out loading or unloading operations.—This is probably the most important safety precaution to observe and *must be strictly adhered to at all times.*

5. Your rocket launching and electrical equipment require even greater care than the other equipment aboard—watch over it and keep it in readiness for that big moment.

Torpedoes.—The big reason why PTs exist. A boat's chief weapon, it gives your boat the wallop of a heavyweight. Every crew member should know his "fish." They are the "lovely ladies" to the torpedoman.

The torpedoman should know his torpedo and launching gear thoroughly; but do not depend on him alone. The case may arise where any officer or man aboard will have to fire torpedos and handle them on deck. First know the launching gear. Understand the operation of the rack and also the remote firing circuits. Know how to start a torpedo manually and how to stop it, and know the tools and their location so that you can lay hands on them immediately.

In preparing a "fully ready" torpedo for firing, the following steps must be taken:

1. Remove the propeller lock.
2. Remove safety pin from the starting toggle.
3. Remove impeller lock on the warhead (on later racks, this is automatic).
4. Remove safety pin from the launching lever (not necessary on the new Mk. 1, Mod. 1 rack).

After completing these steps she is ready to roar to life—and does she roar! ! ! ! Over a ton of hell and destruction for the enemy.

If the launching gear fails, but the torpedo starts we have what is known as a "hot run on deck." This is not only dangerous from the standpoint of giving away your position to the enemy, but the torpedo will throw its turbines through the afterbody shell. This creates a hail of shrapnel on the deck which travels with bullet like force. A man standing near a torpedo when it starts this hot run will have a period of three or four seconds in which he may stop it. This requires a tool #13–14 or #227 in the hand, a quick wit, and an exact knowledge of what to do:

1. Rotate starting index spindle one turn counterclockwise. This will stop the torpedo immediately.
2. Close the main stop valve.
3. Put on propeller lock.
4. See that torpedo is lashed or otherwise secured to the rack. If the tool is not readily available and a man standing by, the torpedo should be let alone. See that all hands stand clear well forward or aft, but do not jump over the side. The warhead will not go off. There is no connection between the after mechanism and the warhead. A torpedo must travel through the water before the warhead is armed.

It is never safe to attempt the stopping of a hot deck run. These accidents may be avoided by frequent dropping of dummy torpedoes from the racks, exercising of the racks with exercising cables which are being provided by the Bureau of Ordnance, and vigilant inspection and lubrication of all moving parts of the rack. It is desirable that the rack be exercised and inspected by competent personnel weekly.

Remember that the thumb screws securing the holding cables should be hand tight and *not wrench tight*. If wrench tight, the hand lever may jam.

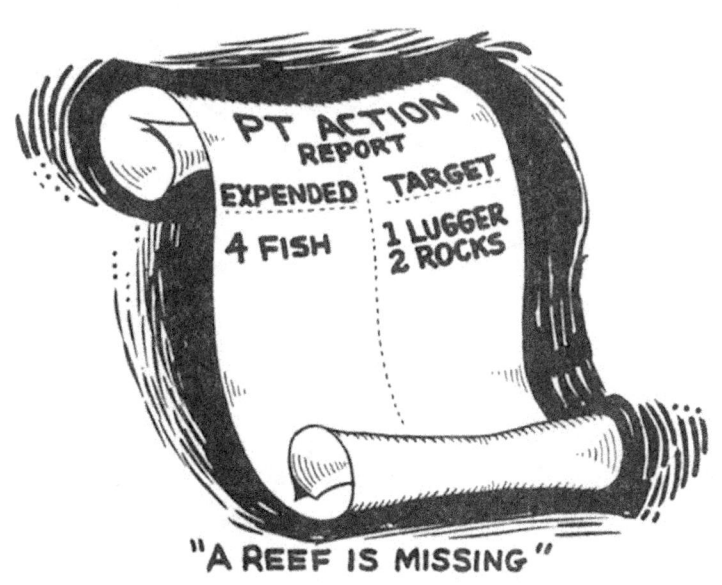

"A REEF IS MISSING"

Small Arms.—Will be in your gunnery locker. Careless handling of these guns has caused many tragedies. Perhaps the major cause of accidents can be traced to failure to take out the clip. Here are the first five rules when you are handing over a gun or tearing it down:

1. Take out the clip!
2. Take out the clip!!
3. Take out the clip!!!
4. Take out the clip!!!!
5. *Take out the clip!!!!!*

FIRE DRILL

The old saying, "Fire is a good servant, but a bad master," applies well to PTs whose wood and gasoline are wonderful ingredients for a roaring fire.

Fire prevention is easily observed on the boats. Just observe all the rules and all will be safe. Every rule and precaution set up by the Navy usually has been originated because of some tragedy in the past.

If an engineer does not want to be a flaming torch of fire, he had better sniff the engine room for gas fumes before he starts the engines or any electrical apparatus in the engine room. Failure to do this has sent more than one PT man to his death. Countless engineers have saved themselves and their shipmates and their boats just by observing this one rule: *Sniff before you turn on any switch!*

Gasoline fumes may be anywhere in the boat. Gasoline and gasoline vapors can flow to any part of the boat through the bilges. A PT looks very peculiar without a charthouse. It happened in Tulagi and two men blew up with it.

"No Smoking Signs" always remind you that you need a smoke very much. Don't be careless. Think of yourself and your shipmates. Observe the no smoking rules.

Refueling is perhaps the most dangerous operation and consequently has the most rules:
1. Know where your CO_2 release valves are.
2. Have your CO_2 bottles topside.
3. Regular Skinner filter funnels are now in use having a ready set-up ground. If, in emergency, you must use the old-type funnel, be sure that you make a good ground for your hose, funnel, and chamois.

4. Have the first-aid kit topside or *on the dock* where you can get to it. No one can go after the kit if it is in the middle of a burning boat.
5. Have as few men on board as possible.
6. Secure all switches.
7. Be sure all breakages in your bonding system are repaired.
8. Flow of gas must cease before you disconnect grounding wires.
9. Of course, the smoking lamp is out.

Any added precautions that you learn from your own experience should also be observed and passed along. Be sure that all fire extinguishers, especially the hand ones, are full to capacity. Once used they should be refilled as soon as possible even though only one tenth of the bottle was used. Once an extinguisher's seal is broken it should not be trusted for future use.

Fire-fighting equipment on the boat itself should always be supplemented by an I. C. E. pump from the beach. Four such pumps are issued to each squadron. They must be kept in a ready-to-go condition and placed on the fuel dock completely set up. This fire-fighting apparatus combines foam with water, thus making it an ideal smotherer of any type fire.

The Lux Hand trigger-release extinguisher can be used several times without loss from leakage. However, the release valve on your large portable extinguishers is not so reliable. Once the sealing cap is ruptured, the valve cannot be closed tightly enough to hold unexpended gas. The unexpended CO_2 will leak away.

Gas Mask.—Every man in the forward areas is issued a gas mask. Your Navy Mask Mk. III or IV is as fine a mask as there is. As long as you take care of it—it will take care of you. You may never need it, but when you do—brother, you need it badly. When your mask is issued to you, don't lay it aside and forget about it.

1. Try it on—make the proper adjustments for a good fit.
2. Stow your mask in a dry place away from excessive heat.
3. Keep only gas protective equipment in your carrier.
4. Don't sit or sleep on your mask.
5. Inspect your mask regularly for defects.
6. Remember your mask is issued only for protection against war gases.
7. Don't use it when spraying paint.
8. It will not protect you from smoke or carbon monoxide, or any oxygen-deficient area.
9. Gas can come at any time—any place—from any direction—listen and be warned —Be Ready.

"Fight Her Till She Sinks, And Don't give up The Ship"—Lawrence, U. S. N.

ABANDON SHIP DRILL

As in every drill you must know your station and the equipment to take with you. Every man is assigned a station and given responsibility for certain gear. This will differ with every boat. The following is set down in order to emphasize several essential points and matters in the procedure known as "Abandoning Ship".

The prime rule is: "Don't give up the ship." If it is impossible to get your boat off a reef, it should be blown to bits. Leave nothing for the enemy. Demolition outfits should be on each boat. Learn how to use it. Above all, understand the difference between the "time fuse" and "instantaneous fuse". The latter called "Prima Cord" (white or light core) burns at the rate of *20,000 feet per second*. They are distinguished by the color of their cores. The importance of knowing the difference is too obvious to explain here. The "time fuse" (black or dark core) burns at the rate of *30–40 sec. per ft.*, thus 50 feet of safety fuse gives you about 25 minutes to get away. Another distinction is that the time fuse is ignited more easily with a match than the Prima Cord. Prima Cord usually requires a cap to ignite it.

Wearing of life jacket is a natural precaution. Everyone wears a jacket on patrol. Slipping on deck, stepping on loose expended shell casings, and sudden jolts have flung many PT men into the sea. Such an accident is well to discuss here for it is in fact "abandoning ship", though involuntarily. Each man should prepare himself for this possibility. Be prepared. Have your life jacket on, have attached in some manner, a small flashlight waterproofed with rubber sheaths, whistle, a mirror, and your 45-caliber pistol strapped on loaded with a clip of 45-caliber tracer. A knife should always be carried on your person. If so equipped and you fall off over the side you have a variety of signalling gear with which to attract attention to your plight and your position. Stay in the boat's wake and in the same spot, if possible, and start whistling and firing your tracer. The boat on hearing or seeing the noise or flashes will immediately reverse course and pick you up.

It will be unusual for you to go out on patrol alone. There is generally another boat in your vicinity to give assistance. It is possible, though, for both to be disabled at the same time and both must evacuate.

As a rule your boat will be fairly close to land if you meet disaster on a reef, from shore guns, plane bombing, or naval gunnery. To reach land all you need is a fairly accurate knowledge of your position, a compass and a chart or map. The officer in charge should give the general course (South or NE, or W, etc.), to the base or friendly shore. Then if separated each can strike in the proper direction. It is best to stick together, however, for in numbers there is greater safety. Each man on board will be responsible for certain kinds of gear to haul along. A list can be made out from the following, but first let us go through the whole procedure.

After every possible effort to save your boat has failed, your first duty is to complete your destruction bill. That is, destroy all confidential gear beyond recognition and other gear beyond repair. It is wise to always have your publications in a weighted canvas bag or sack and throw them off *only in deep water*. This drill is fully as important as the Abandon Ship Drill. Run them in conjunction for practice to insure complete familiarity with the duty assigned. For complete details on Destruction Bill see pp. 46–48 MTB Communications Manual. The value of this publication cannot be overestimated.

Before going over the side be sure you have all necessary gear lashed inside the liferafts. Most important, have a painter (small line secured from the bow of the raft to the PT). This will prevent the raft from drifting away.

Don't forget your clips of 45 cal. tracer. A gun without ammunition is merely a club and you can pick a club up anywhere in the jungle.

More pointers: Keep your clothes on and especially your shoes. Keep your hair dry, that is, don't jump into the water, just slide in. Don't get into the raft. It is primarily a support and not a sail boat.

In addition to the balsa raft, each boat is equipped with two 7-man rubber rafts which are ideal for abandoning ship. They are lightweight equipment and not designed to be used as dinghies. Maintain them for the one important purpose for which they are issued—*Life Saving*.

FOR THAT BIG MOMENT

It is beyond the scope of the publication to discuss the tactical use of PTs, yet such an important phase of PTs mission cannot be overlooked. The interested reader, that is, those who are supposed to know this phase of PT operation are referred to the excellent publication, MTB Current Tactical Orders and Doctrine, 1945, U. S. F. (Confidential).

The ability of your boat is amazing. This versatility has gained for it an important part in the fleet. To know what is expected of PTs and what you will be doing with them, do not fail to gain all the dope that's necessary to the operation of your boat. Get it from your O. N. I. officer.

Remember it's the simple, common-sense things that are important. Plenty will depend on your spunk and nerve. It always helps to note that your boat is far superior to anything near its size. You have the best equipment available. With this knowledge should come the confidence that *you with your boat* can outgun, outmaneuver, outrun, outfight, any comparable enemy and often a much larger enemy. PT men need not be urged to fight—it's their routine. That's why they are in PTs because they *can* fight and want to.

One last word about combat. *Know your recognition procedure.* This is important knowledge for everyone on the boat. Study our planes and ships and those of the enemy. Check all intelligence dope before you go out on patrol. You may be able to sneak up on a Jap barge but don't try it with one of Uncle Sammie's Dreadnaughts. Know your enemy and your friends.

"JAP IN A FIX"

GEAR TO TAKE TO THE AREA

This section has been inserted by request of countless men about to leave for the war zone. Here it is. Make the most of it.

The listing that follows is not complete but it does give a good basis for packing your sea bag, though not all the gear listed is essential. Emphasis is placed on items which will add to your safety, cleanliness, comfort, and well-being. The list follows, in the raw:

Necessities:

12 sets underwear.
12 pairs each of black and white socks.
4 trousers (dungarees, etc.).
6 shirts.
2 pairs of shoes.
Sewing kit.
Swimming trunks.
Shoestrings.
6 towels.
12 handkerchiefs.
Shaving gear and toilet articles.
Scrub brush.

Good to have:

Soap box for soap (good to keep cigarettes dry).
Hand mirror that will not rust.
Games.
Educational correspondence courses.
Sun glasses.
Small pocket compass (with magnifying glass if possible).
Waterproof watch. (Don't ruin your good watch.)
Extra watch straps.
Knife.
Flashlight.
Sneakers and moccasins.
Lighter with flints and wicks.
Band aids.
Maps.

Cheap canvas luggage (will not rot or mildew as rapidly as leather and is lighter).
Fountain pen.
Fishing tackle. (Some outfits take some for the whole squadron.)
Ear plugs (engine room noise and swimming).
Padlock (combination if possible).
Books.
World Almanac. (One on every boat will settle many arguments.)
Address book.

Settle these before leaving:

Have insurance and will squared away.
Check your allotments.
Give power-of-attorney to trustworthy person.

Comments.—White socks are essential to foot hygiene. You will do most of your own laundry, so get a Kiyi brush. Soap, shaving gear (except razors) are usually available. The best watch straps are canvas (no metal parts). Carry a couple. An extra seabag may be used to send home excess gear or souvenirs.

A knife is carried by every good sailor. The whistle and reflector are useful in signaling. Have a compass to find your way if you are in the jungle or adrift in a raft. The magnifying glass can be used to start a fire. Put your name on the canteen issued to you. Keep it on your web belt for going over the side and have it full of water. Flashlights are always useful. Put one in your life jacket.

You will probably be out of the States a good many months. *Do not waste this time.* Learn something. Knowledge is valuable, and acquiring it will make time go faster. Correspondence courses are open to you in almost any subject that interests you. You may earn high-school and college credits through this medium. See your educational officer or write to the USAFI (U. S. Armed Forces Institute), Madison, Wisconsin.

Diving masks can give great pleasure. There is a whole new world of fantastic beauty open to you a few feet below the water's surface. A mask will increase your swimming pleasure 100 percent.

After it is issued to you, keep your own life jacket. Stow in it the suggested signaling gear. Keep it clean; and dry it out every day. A wet, soggy jacket will bring you to the bottom instead of to the top. Hang it in an up-side down position.

Fountain pens are difficult to get these days. Take care of the one you have. A song session is always welcome under a South Sea moon. Take a musical instrument if it can stand the gaff. Ear plugs are helpful in preventing fungus infection.

Moccasins are easy to get on if you're in a sack when an air raid sounds. Sneakers are good for coral fishing. Band aids are always helpful. Maps of the world to keep you up with the war and for general interest. Maybe you can prove to the boys that Sheboygan is on the map. Books on geography are surprisingly interesting. Games will help to pass the hours. Always try to set up a tournament or competition. It is much more fun this way and the pleasure is lasting. Allot most of your money so you will not get caught or tempted by the card sharks and dice shooters. Swiss files and chisels or any similar small tools are a great help in smoothing out souvenirs. Song books are good.

Appoint a trustworthy lawyer or an intelligent trustworthy friend to take care of things which may come up during your absence (e. g. if you inherited property from a wealthy relative while across). Square away your finances before you go away. It will save you a lot of headaches and worry. Rather than depending on money orders, which are often hard to get, set up a checking account so you can send presents home and pay small bills.

HEALTH NOTES

The secret of keeping healthy in the tropics is primarily, *be clean!* Likewise, observe all the health requirements put out by your squadron doctor. If you want to die or want to get that I-want-to-die feeling, just fail to take your anti-malaria doses. Malaria is the chief threat to your health not only in the area but in later life. You may not seem to have malaria while in the combat zone, but when you come home, it is liable to come out openly. Ask a few vets. They know. Take your medicine and be glad that it is available.

Fungus infections are very prevalent in the Area. They are most uncomfortable and can lead to serious impairment of hearing, breathing, sight, and manual dexterity.

Athlete's foot is the usual ailment. This disease appears generally on the feet (between the toes) at first. Then it travels up the legs to the crotch, armpits, hands, and eyes. The scratching irritation is terrific and the raw sores created by scratching are excellent entry spots for other foreign bacteria causing serious complications. *Prevention is the best advice.* Wear white socks and air your feet often. Men on patrol sometimes go 2 or 3 days without taking off their shoes. The dampness, sweating, and spray keep their feet continuously wet and without air. Your feet must breathe. Take your shoes and socks off at least every 24 hours. Dry them out and put on dry footwear. Holes cut in marine shoes and in sneakers have helped numerous such cases. Ventilate your feet, expose them to the sun's rays occasionally. Dry them well—especially between the toes.

Watch out for ticks picked up in the jungle and watch, too, for other lice which might get on your body (especially in the crotch, armpits, and between the toes.) They may be sucking your blood and injecting a disease into you for hours unless you inspect your body for them. A tick or sucker should not be yanked off. He may leave his "stinger" in you. Rather touch it with a lighted cigarette or a drop of iodine or alcohol. It will then probably drop or squirm off.

Men living ashore should keep their mosquito netting tucked under the mattress. If it is not, mosquitoes, snakes, scorpions, centipedes, and other venomous creatures can get in. Shake and check your blankets before you turn in.

Preparations for those already having the infection are available at sick bay. Make use of the knowledge that will save you much pain and sleep. Follow the instructions on the bottle!!! If you do not, you will be walking on a mass of sores which often break out on the soles of the feet. For an object lesson, go into a sick bay in the Area and see the poor blokes that failed to observe the rules. Some are strung up like cripples and covered from head to foot with violet paint. Others, more fortunate, will be seen limping around.

Swimming is great exercise and there are zones prescribed for it. Always swim in pairs. This precaution for safety is too obvious to be explained. There have been instances where giant clams have held men below the water for an uncomfortably long time. Thick vegetation, seaweed, lines and submerged trees may tangle one man up. Rocks and "nigger heads" have stunned many men.

Incidents mentioned above are not so common as the infections that can be acquired from swimming in tropical waters. Salt water in this region is usually very unsanitary. It is teeming with minute organisms and slime. Do not use it to wash out cuts or sores. It will probably make them worse. Ear fungus is perhaps the most prevalent malady contracted from swimmimg. Prevent it by wearing ear plugs and by drying out your ears completely after coming out. If you have any irritation, growth, or pain go to sick bay.

Cold fresh water in a lake or mountain stream looks wonderful, but it may be harmful. Tropical fresh water, unless treated (chlorinated) properly, is dangerous both for drinking and bathing. Swim only in water approved by the sanitation officer or medical officer.

Chlorinated water is not pleasant to taste. However, there are now available "chlorination kits" which purify the water without leaving that chlorine taste. Get one for your boat. Fresh water tanks should be inspected. If any unusual growths or barnacles or "animals" are found report it to sick bay.

Jungle sores or ulcers are as dirty and uncomfortable as they sound. "Tulagi rot" is another nonmedical name for this ailment. How they start is not quite evident. The precautions that follow may be helpful. Treat all sores and scratches (especially coral scratches) immediately with iodine or mercurochrome or alcohol. Dress it and do not go swimming. Keep clean by washing with fresh sanitary water and soap. Wash your clothes frequently.

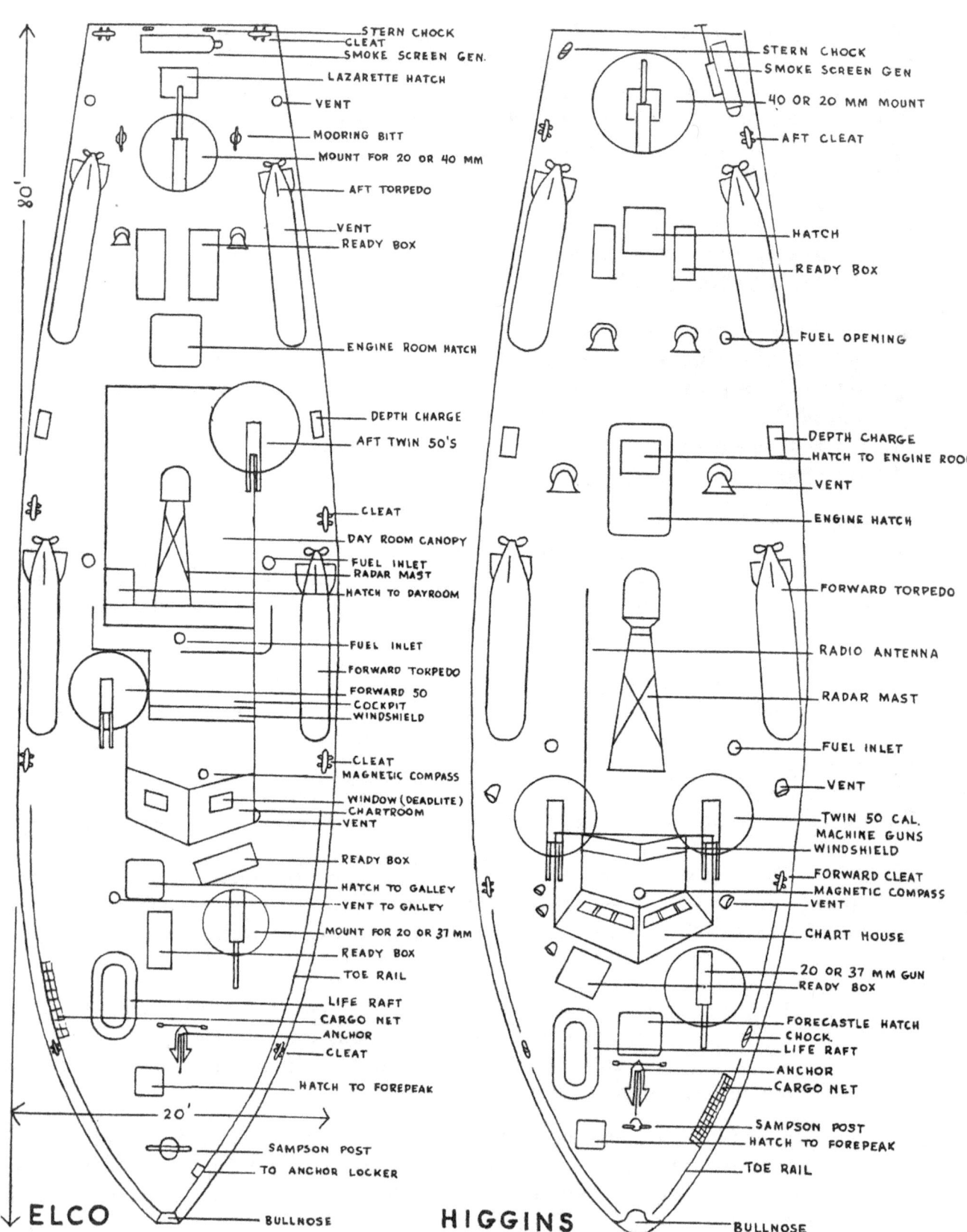

©2010 PERISCOPE FILM LLC
ALL RIGHTS RESERVED
ISBN #978-1-935700-17-3
WWW.PERISCOPEFILM.COM

THE FLEET TYPE SUBMARINE SERIES

Now Available!

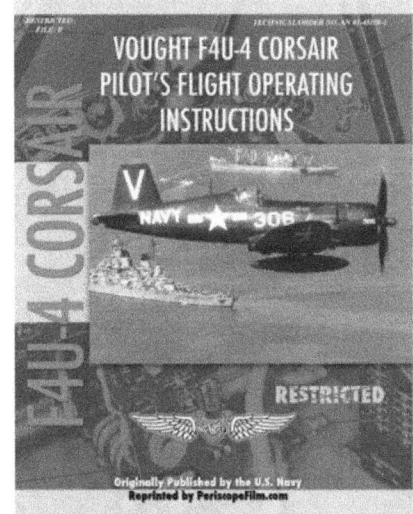
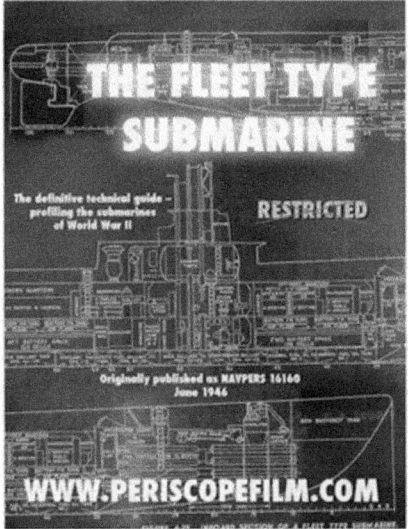
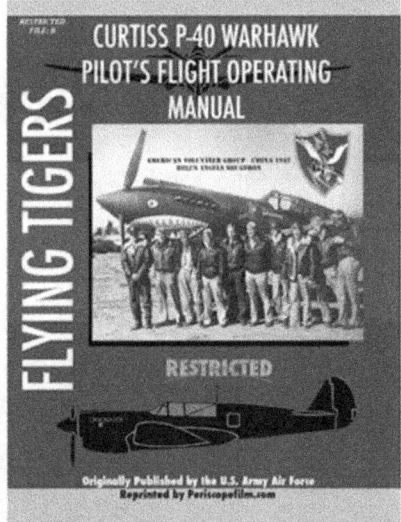

ALSO NOW AVAILABLE
FROM PERISCOPEFILM.COM

Warships DVD Series

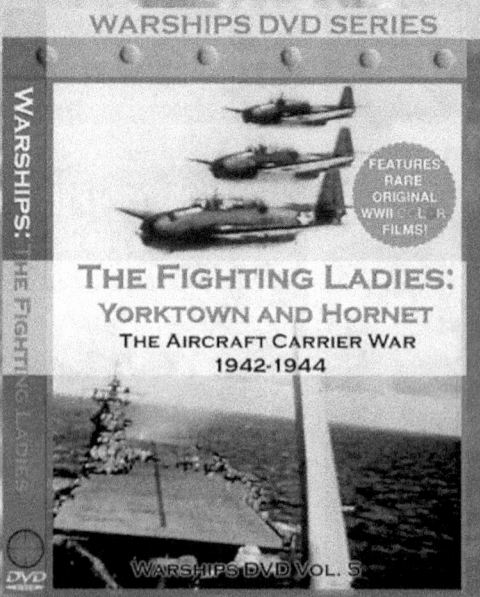

Now Available!

www.ingramcontent.com/pod-product-compliance
Lightning Source LLC
LaVergne TN
LVHW061347060426
835512LV00012B/2597